DIVINE ATTENTION

DIVINE ATTENTION

poems by

PAULETTE ROESKE

1995

Louisiana State University Press
Baton Rouge and London

Again, for Addie
this only daughter

Manufactured in the United States of America
First printing
04 03 02 01 00 99 98 97 96 95   5 4 3 2 1
Designer: Glynnis Phoebe
Typeface: Granjon
Typesetter: Moran Printing, Inc.
Printer and binder: Thomson-Shore, Inc.

Library of Congress Cataloging-in-Publication Data
Roeske, Paulette.
    Divine attention : poems / by Paulette Roeske.
        p.   cm.
    ISBN 0-8071-1950-4. — ISBN 0-8071-1951-2 (pbk.)
    I. Title.
PS3568.0367D58   1995
811'.54—dc20   94-38208
                                                                CIP

The author offers grateful acknowledgment to the editors of publications in which poems in this volume previously appeared, some in slightly different form: "The Absence of Edges" and "High Image Therapy" in *Poetry Northwest* (Summer, 1994); "Accordion" in *Poetry East*, (Spring, 1994); "Tournament of Destruction" in *Virginia Quarterly Review*, LXIX (Winter, 1993); "Deep Sex" in *Seattle Review*, XV (Spring/Summer, 1992); "The Ecstasy of St. Theresa" in *Willow Springs*, XXIX (Winter, 1991); "Preparing the Dead" in *Zone 3*, VI (Fall, 1991); "The Shock Ward" and "The Wife Takes a Child" in *Spoon River Quarterly*, XVI (Summer/Fall, 1991); "In Sympathy, My Daughter Sleeps Beside Me" in *Warren Wilson Review*, II (Summer, 1991): "Childhood Friend, Thirty Years Later" and "Family Tree" in *Louisiana Literature*, VIII (Spring, 1991); "Mother and Child" in *Poets On*, XV (Winter, 1991); "Divine Attention" in *Whetstone*, VI (1989); "The Deaf Girl Studies Poetry" in *Whetstone*, V (1988); "Duet" in *South Coast Poetry Journal*, VI (Fall, 1988); "The Body Can Ascend No Higher," in *Chester H. Jones Foundation National Poetry Competition Winners, 1990* (Chardon, Ohio, 1990); "Divine Attention," "the Shock Ward," "Mother and Child," "Duet," "the Deaf Girl Studies Poetry," "Preparing the Dead," "The Body Can Ascend No Higher," "Childhood Friend, Thirty Years Later," "The Wife Takes a Child," "Family Tree," and *"The Ecstasy of St. Theresa,"* in *The Body Can Ascend No Higher* (Normal, Ill.: Illinois Writers, Inc., 1992).

The author also wishes to thank the Illinois Arts Council, Ragdale Foundation, and the College of Lake County for support during the time some of these poems were written.

Publication of this book has been supported by a grant from the National Endowment for the Arts in Washington, D.C., a federal agency.

The paper in the book meets the guidelines for permanence and durability of the Committee on Production Guidelines for Book Longevity of the Council on Library Resources. ∞

We walk with one foot in each world
—*Charles Wright*

The Soul selects her own Society—
—*Emily Dickinson*

CONTENTS

I

DIVINE ATTENTION

I

The Board of Education had its reasons
for sending me across the racial border
into the ramshackle high school
where I would grapple with street gangs
on the turf of remedial English.
On day one in the dust-covered classroom,
shot-out windows admitting jigsaw pieces
of true sky, I learned the meaning of anarchy.
At the first bell, Rat shook up
a bottle of Pepsi and sprayed Weasel,
then someone snatched a tampon from DeeDee's purse
for a game of catch. In the front row,
with divine attention, Carmen painted
her nails chartreuse. I pounded the textbook
on the desk, a trick I stole from Khrushchev.

Day after day I followed the carefully
prepared script the Board believed would open
closed doors. Diagrammed sentences
marched across the blackboard like stick figures
in a learn-to-draw-me book. While I droned
about the parts of speech, on the bulletin board
they posted the school news—who bore
what baby, who held up which gas station or
corner store, which gang crossed what line,
who bled from what wound, who was arrested,
who arraigned, who sent up the river,
who checked in at the morgue.

The day a brick crashed through
the last whole window,
I told the class we were lucky
no one was killed and to leave
the glass on the floor.
William, myopic, overweight, a bully,
picked up the biggest shard
and entered the center aisle, testing
the point on his palm. The world
was Fat William, slow-stepping
down the collision course, and me,
adrift beside the small island
of my desk. When he reached the front,
he raised his arms inch
by inch above his head, forty-five
pairs of eyes climbing after him.
Stretched like a victim on the rack,
he paused. Lost in the wavering
pools of his magnified eyes,
I didn't will his hand
away from the soft edges
I call me, nor did I invite it.
As for him, he must have guessed how little
the difference between cutting
me and cutting himself.
With an angry sleight of hand
he brought down the glass
at my feet.

3

When I wore the black mini-skirt
and black and white striped blouse,
puffed sleeves buttoned to my forearms
like gauntlets, red bow draped at my neck,
DeeDee said she liked my dress.
From her purse she fished
a well-thumbed copy of *Glamour* stamped
DO NOT REMOVE. Women—thin, white,
too happy—rose from the clutter
of candy wrappers, crushed cigarette packs,
action comics, cosmetics swept straight
from the shelf into DeeDee's purse.
The women summed up her dog-eared
ambition. She tortured her hair
blonde and powdered her face as if
to erase herself. Again she said, "I like
your dress." In the next row, Carmen
added another point to the black star
she was painting on her thumbnail.
Without glancing up, she said, "So? She got
a job. She working." DeeDee said she wanted
my dress. I imagined myself naked
in front of the class as in those dreams
teachers sometimes have. I imagined her
as me, the red bow in a stranglehold
around her neck.

4

"Hey, white girl, the name's Rat.
I'm a poet. I'm crazy," he said,
leaping onto my desk, executing

a soft-shoe that broke pencils
and footprinted the detailed
records required by the State.
"That's Mrs. to you," I said. "You're
no more crazy than I am. And
get off my desk." Barely clearing
Carmen's bowed head, he jumped
from one nailed-down desk
to the next until he reached
the door at the back of the room.

On the school's one reluctant
mimeograph machine, I cranked out
copies of poems signed *One Crazy Rat*.
Purple smudges bruised every page.
Personally he handed them out
to the thirty students left,
saying, "I'm a poet. I'm famous.
And her? She Mrs. White Girl." He
didn't come back after that day.
Maybe he turned sixteen, maybe
he turned his back at the wrong
time, or maybe he figured that day
was as good as life got and
how much wiser to bow out
with both barrels smoking. Daily
I checked the bulletin board for news.

5

During the strike the teachers
called me scab and worse, but Weasel
ditched class to guard my car.
I could see him from the window,

lounging on the hood of my Chevy,
rolling joints. By then I had thrown away
the script and spent the days
reinventing my favorite books—talking up
Kurtz's crimes in the Congo,
ascribing to him tortures borrowed
from the Bible, Dante, and de Sade.
Iago was misunderstood, cried the twelve
who remained, and the Minotaur
merely confused by his odd
combination of hands and hooves.
They warmed to the world where everything
is permitted, believing at last
they could imitate art in their lives.

6

After school in the girls' john,
alone among the ineradicable
odors of urine, smoke, and lilac cologne,
where lipsticked walls cursed
honkies, pigs, spicks, the fucked-over world,
where cracked plaster leaked roaches
and forgotten books spilled their undecipherable formulas
beside the overflowing toilets,
I abandoned the false metaphor
calling life a blank slate.
For a year I had watched them turn
desecrated page after desecrated page
even though they already knew no idea
is ever whole or pure
and salvation is a profane word.

THE SHOCK WARD

Saint Anthony's Hospital

Convinced at sixteen my future
lay in Africa nursing natives,
already dreaming my sincere face
into group pictures, already wearing
the impeccable whites naming me angel,
I applied as a part-time nurse's aide
to get a jump on goodness.

Hoping at the very least
for contagious diseases, instead
I was buzzed behind the double set
of locked doors where clock time faltered
and reality answered to many names.
Frances met me with pots of ivy
she carried all day from window
to window, searching out the last
slant of winter light.
In the recreation room, Esther
picked the bandages on her wrists
into ribbons, their sad frivolity
trailing the hands that aligned
the magazines spine against spine
or fanned them like unlucky cards.
Richard turned the sofas upside down
for trenches. He hid matches
in his socks and built fires
fueled with Esther's magazines
and the belief he had been called to war.

I was paid to play "Blueberry Hill"
on the piano and encourage

Frances, Richard, and the rest
to sing along. Sometimes
we made Popsicle-stick trinket boxes
or braided keychains from strips
of red, white, and blue plastic,
but no one was allowed trinkets
or keys. A girl my age rocked on the edge
of her bed. When she couldn't stop
screaming, they whispered
her into the shock room
where the oversized chair
rigged with straps and wires
took up nearly all the space.
They counted on the chair
to make Frances leave
the plants in their proper places,
to make Richard forget
where he stashed his matches.
Everyone forgot the words
to "Blueberry Hill" and which color
belongs between red and blue.

On treatment days I sat alone
at the piano. Outside, icicles
grew into spears and snow-blind cars
grazed the parking lot. On another
continent, natives who had never
braced their nerves
against the electric whir
or watched their world turn white,
dropped their guard
and held out their arms to me.

Tournament of Destruction

No one's here for the polite processional
and so we cheer the sudden end of protocol
when drivers rev their souped-up engines
in a look-at-me strut,
firing as unpredictably as love.
Slowly the red sky darkens.
Lights go up around the oval track
like the circuitry of sexual excitement
waking the nerves. When the serious music
of speed begins, thousands
of cubic inches of adulterated power
vibrate the wooden bleachers
and every paying customer
tracks its course up his spine,
up and around the thrilled muscle
of his heart. Crazily
the cars blur sideways into the first curve,
pitching fist-sized chunks of clay
off the track, and obligingly
you lean into me. That, too, addresses my heart
like your absence when you lean away
as you must at the next curve,
the warm rub of shoulder to shoulder
gone suddenly cool. The cars circle
in dust so thick we eat it, take it in
to veil the eye, torment the inner ear,
and I think how we, too, repeat
our ceremony of injury.

Little wonder this place speaks to you,
you who are never anywhere except in motion,
you who cannot get enough of speed,
you with your habit of anarchy—

no sleep, bad food, the reckless
disarray you call home, no wonder
you understand the object
is not catch and hold but chase and pass
after the brief neck and neck of parallels
as again one car slips up against another
and they touch down the full length
of their bodies and race that way at breakneck speed
until metal tears like paper
calling into question an old idea of safety
and one of them pulls free
with only the track ahead,
blank as the sky, unbridled.

A Child of Divorce, Her Father, and Her Father's Lover

Under a moon neatly halved,
under the oak whose branches complicate the sky,
they sit on the back steps, this father
and the woman he loves.
Late, late into the summer night
she leans against his body
which yields to her bones.
Can they help it if their hands
have a mind of their own
or that a thing so vast as the night
drops suddenly away? As for the house,

call it the other side of the moon.
The dining room's dark walls
close down around the child alone at the table.
On the chandelier above her,
four brass swans rise from their brassy swamp
craning their necks past the oval globes
that throw 300 watts on the little girl,
bleary with need, who labors over crayons
to draw what she cannot say she wants:

the figure of a woman locked in a tower
without windows, without doors,
a woman unrescuable in this tower so narrow
her crucified arms address stone.
A princess, yes, but unbeautiful,
her eyes two empty cups,
her face the mask we call tragedy,
her prince a profound absence
gone off in search of his lost daughter.

No matter, for the woman cannot escape
even the black web of her hair,
tangled as wire, a crown of wire,
a heavy crown that pushes her head
down into her dress. Of course it's red—
the dress that cuffs her wrists,
hobbles her ankles—like the sun,
high in one corner,
that should warm stone and the hole
where the woman's heart should be.

Preparing the Dead

After high school Latin class,
I put on the yellow pinafore
of the employee-of-least-consequence
and drove to Mrs. Goetzman,
paralyzed for forty years,
who taught me how to turn
her body and arrange the feather
pillows along her spine,
and to Bud, blind from birth,
who translated my features,
his tentative fingers on my eyelids and lips
etching out another me,
and who, brushing back my hair
he said felt black,
concluded, "You are beautiful."

In the broom closet at break time,
Virginia and Lucille, others of my caste,
black women double and triple my age,
joked about the dim logic
and lapsed etiquette of the lifers
on the ward. Virginia handed out
Lucky Strikes all around.
Among the mops and wringer pails,
eye-smarting antiseptics,
and in a space so small
we stood hip to hip,
we smoked ourselves blue.
It was Lucille, swaybacked,
gap-toothed, who schooled me
in the preparation of the dead.

Sanctioned to open the door
posted KEEP OUT, she ushered
me into a scene larger than conjugations
or textbook formulas.
We would work our inexact science
in eerie half-light, the late
afternoon sun through the gauze curtains
washing ceiling, floor, walls,
the draped figure, everything
the same hospital green.
Whipping back the sheet
like a magician uncovering a prop,
Lucille uncovered Bud, blind eyes
unweighted, naked as birth.
The green light settled on his body,
plump as a lapdog's. His bald head
shone like a third eye.

We took our positions,
one on each side, like angels
conspiring at the gate.
From the hospital-issue death kit,
Lucille removed a roll of cotton wadding.
Crossing herself before she crossed Bud's legs,
one well-placed push flipped him
on his side. I held his wrists
while Lucille packed his rectum.

In silence we washed his face,
neck, arms, chest. The only sound,
ordinary tap water sloshing
in the porcelain basin.
Over his round stomach,
down toward the frazzled white hair
fringing his abdomen, it was there
I hesitated. With thumb and forefinger
Lucille lifted his penis
onto her palm. She kneaded

it slowly, deliberately, her private test
for some last vital sign. Admitting
the doctors were right, she sucked
her teeth then added men were maddened
by that little animal. She told me
I was getting old enough
to know the calming trick with spoons
(silver is best) and what code
to tap against its head. Thighs,
calves, ankles, feet, we rolled
him over and began again.

Lucille assured me his soul
was loose in the room, one among legions
come to lead Bud to the next world.
"Girl," she said, "they all around us.
Keep your arms close at your sides.
Don't crowd." I searched the air
for something elusive as smoke or feathers,
as fingers brushing back my hair
but returned to the irrefutable iron bed,
the starched sheets, to one hand
capable of holding the other.

In indelible ink I printed
Bud's name on a luggage tag
and looped the thread three times
around his toe. We eased the crinkly paper bag
down past his bald head, blind eyes,
past every newly washed part of him,
then Lucille pulled the drawstring
tight, and tied a double bow.

"Sleeping Beauty":
An Alternative Reading

Consider the prince a blunderer
who by dumb luck chose the day the spell expired
but somehow believed it was for him
the thorns blossomed and parted.
What imbecilic tune did he hum as he wandered
toward the castle, dragging his sword
like a tail? Round-cheeked, gap-toothed,
plump as a hen, he waltzed down the path
toward the end of his days. He got what
he thought he wanted: the scene set in motion,
the *My hero, come at last!* without wondering

what sleeper would celebrate the end
of a hundred years of dreaming or frame
with mortal lips the wish to be kissed back
to meat blackening on the spit,
the sticky legs of flies,
the shit-bejeweled barnyard where a brainless
black hen squawks under the axe
and horse and hound protest flea, tick,
every species of lice known and unknown,
the bacterial soup of all hungers
and their consequences.

Call them the lucky ones,
those other sons of kings hung out like laundry
on a rack of thorns. Never mind
how they were caught and held
by the million bitter fingers
or their miserable deaths. Call theirs
the happy ending: a trip to oblivion

spurred by wild imaginings: their lips
on the lips of beauty,
a kiss they will hold forever.   .

The Body Can Ascend No Higher

Capuchin Catacombs, Palermo

Hung up on hooks,
they lean from their niches, these thousands,
each with something to show—
top hat, Count Dracula cloak,
Jesus beard, two blue eyes
dry as eggs. Someone
has planned this party,
rigged the monk with a broomstick spine,
the bride with breasts of straw.
In a high alcove, an unascribable breeze
lifts the veil from a seventeenth-century face
that mocks the old promise: *dust to dust.*

But how they tire of the dry
preserving air, immovable hand
falling short of what itch, the generations
trooping past arrayed in the dress of the times—
those mirrors they stare back at,
showing how the world has not changed,
chaining them to their lives
as they would have led them.

II

DUET

She always chooses *primo,*
the ascending melody airy
as her adolescence. I take *secondo,*
providing the chords' deep balance.
Right foot forward, left
behind, level wrists, we lift
our shoulders in unison
then drop them like a sigh,
our signal to begin.

Following Diabelli's script,
our hands explore the opposite
poles of bass and treble clefs
or nearly brush.
Twenty fingers reassembling
like wrens in the yard's border
of burning bush.
A passerby, walking his dog
or searching out comfort
in the night sky, glances
through the lit window.
Drawn by the pure notes,
he remains to admire
the young girl,
her fair skin and storybook
hair, her straight back,
her neck's intelligent curve.
The dark figure beside her
doubling every vertical, every arc,
he mistakes for shadow.

How can I quarrel with his assumption,
so gratified by this shared language,
this dialogue in four hands
practiced in the art
of question and answer,
this shoulder against mine,
this only daughter.

MOTHER AND CHILD

Mary's breasts are as full
as if she were nursing the grown son
sprawled across her knees.
If he were a baby,
she would fret about the ladder of his ribs
her hand would have climbed
to lodge in the pit under his right arm,
a niche shaped for a hand.
Already leaned and leaning
away from the mother who housed him,
without it he would surely slip,
following the incline of his dropped arm,
dropped hip, head already turned toward the future.
Lost as she is in yards of drapery,
the bit of hitched-up hem
beneath those splayed fingers
denies, as only a mother could,
the unbearable fact. The fingers
of her other hand, palm up at her side,
unfold like a question.
Not one pore of her body
touches the body of her dead son.

In the cathedral I photograph
the photographer photographing *The Pietà,*
his presence proving the mother larger than life
as if swollen with mourning.
Imagine a finger laid on an open eye,
on the flayed body of the saint
who carries his skin like a coat over one arm,
on the heart unanchored
torn from the only home it has known.

I say I am nearly done with mothering,
my daughter grown, but what do I know?
After dinner I still take her leg-numbing weight
onto my knees in the ladderback chair,
a holding ritual begun before birth,
and in our ritual silence,
the candles still lit,
I call up frame after frame
in which she is fatherless, limp with fever,
her child's body draped with whole towels
soaked in the ice-filled basin,
her eyes blank as coins
kissed for hope, kissed for luck,
as if such kisses could conjure
mercy's invisible hand.
See where memory takes a mother
who stands before the sculptor's account of deep loss,
praying the prayer she knows
without being taught.

FAMILY TREE

> To speak of the dead is to make
> them live again:
>
> we invent what we need.
> —*Charles Wright*

Thumbing through the centuries,
this web of begats spun by a stranger
who claims he's the distant relation
of a distant relation,
I suspect his long suit
was imagination, the names culled
from rare novels or the Ouija board
pressed into service.
So we began, he concludes, in Saxony,
1695, and end on page 11
with my daughter's name
misspelled, a blank following
the year of her birth.

Stuck under the back cover,
I find an envelope addressed
in my grandmother's hand.
Inside, obituaries naming
Charles who served in the Civil War
and survived to die of old age.
And Little Alberta dead at twelve
who *was perfectly reconciled*
to depart to that world beyond the skies
where there are no changes
or separations. But
there is no speculation
about Frederick's last thoughts
when he leapt from the scaffold,
and grandmother's three infant sons
go unnamed.

The dead cannot rest
thus reduced to a list
like an order for groceries,
but there is no one left
who remembers Charles's round face,
bland, boyish, his embarrassed
smile dimpling one cheek.
And no one ever knew
Alberta was dreaming of Christmas
when the white wall to the other
world opened. In her dream
she wore the blue satin dress
she had always wanted,
a paper rose tucked in the sash.
For Frederick, the long descent
unfolded leisurely as snow. He drifted
through a vision of a hundred parachutes
hung above a beach like a field
of white poppies. In the field,
three babies, their identical stillborn faces
featureless but fully formed.
For them I choose names
I would have given the sons
I never bore. Luke, Jake, Mark,
hardy names grafted onto their frail frames.

After all the names and faces,
the twentieth century ends
with my daughter, now a young woman,
a beauty with a dimple high on one cheek,
blue her favorite color, hers
the only name I've offered for the list,
and me, entering middle age,
again opening the envelope,
finding among the fragile scraps
a lock of hair, a shade
that matched my own, a curl
tied with red thread soft as the names

Emma, Amelia, Marie,
and a ticket to the World's
Columbian Exposition,
October 9th, 1893,
a child's ticket,
the one Alberta didn't need.

In Sympathy, My Daughter
Sleeps Beside Me

The laser did not address her flesh
and after all it's a small affair,
the offending part an insult
vaporized by a beam of light.
When they wheel me back to the room,
only a single needle in my hand
feeds its sleepy solution
in a prudent drip. What's so frightening
about that? But understand
my daughter's been waiting
and she's at that sensitive age
between wanting a mother
and wishing her lost in a country
with an unpronounceable name.

Once we are alone,
I watch her face abandon scorn.
When need creeps in,
I invite her to lie beside me
in the narrow hospital bed
and sleep compels us both
into its realm, each for our own
reasons. Sleep, a woman
in a white dress, kind, omniscient,
who has known us forever,
synchronizes our breath—mother and daughter,
wounded and well, touched
by the same failing light,
taking in the same air.
On the single pillow as we sleep
the blond strands of her long hair

travel of their own accord
toward the dark nest of my dark hair,
and her fingers drift
into the palm of my good hand.

As If

in the Serbian Cemetery

Not Serbs, not mourners,
we puzzle out the Cyrillic alphabet,
invent lives for the faces
fixed on the headstones
in white ceramic frames
as if, like the four-eyed fish,
they watch above and below the surface.
Filigreed, finely wrought,
these garden chairs are not meant for us,
nor the child's plot-turned-park
with picnic table and bench
scaled to her size.

During this summer of drought
the hot wind rains down on us—
you who are not my mother
but the one I would choose
if choice were possible,
and me.
      Row after row
deeper into the acred crosses
we walk as if our destination
were not memory:
for you, your parents,
for me, August, 1972,
when I lingered at the lip
of my grandmother's open grave—
she who was first loved, the one
I called mother—and the day turned
like the foetus in my womb. Lost
on the long plateau between the unborn
and the new dead, my eyes ricocheted

off the horizon, as if the surface
were the only dimension, as if
sky, field, and ocean were stone,
as if the body were stone.

Too many days of blistering heat
and the graves run to ruin, the lanterns,
their eternal flames gone out.
Imagine then how willingly
we scan the darkening sky,
welcome the air's vague music.
You describe a German film
about angels who return
to those who need them.
Around us they rise up: hands
of the soldier, the musician's hands
curved on the fret, hands of the monk,
the child, the last king
of Yugoslavia.
                    In your poem
you wish your parents into stars.
How they shimmer, grow brighter,
like the air after this storm,
pure, boundless,
that carries the one word
you speak to me: *daughter.*

ACCORDION

I

My father's had a diamond
on the button he told me was middle C,
the one button I could name
among the hundred black buttons
set in mother-of-pearl,
buttons small as fish eyes
crowding each other like children.
And so I marveled when his broad fingers
blunt as hammers chose and impeccably sounded
"The Beer Barrel Polka,"
the tune my sister and I begged for
as we romped in the rec room,
our faces washed in ruddy light
from the Schlitz sign behind the knotty pine
bar, our fingers interlocked
as we galloped the breathy stumble of foals.

Sundays after roast beef, mashed potatoes,
white bread—everything sopped in gravy,
custard pie flecked with nutmeg, and
long after the interminable sermons he slept through,
my sister on one side, me on the other
to stall trouble, still we wriggled in the pew
anticipating the hour our father
would hoist his accordion from its velvet-lined case,
slip the thick leather straps over his shoulders,
unsnap the bellows and play that curious machine—
part piano upended, the only familiar part

besides the diamond—play with eyes closed
sheet music from the '30s and '40s
which pictured on their covers beautiful women,
dewey eyed, in the arms of men
whose raked-back hair immortalized
teeth tracks from their combs. Suave,
I might have called them, with longing.

He played standing up, or down on one knee
as if he were about to propose
marriage to someone as stunning as my mother
when she was photographed in her white
nurse's uniform, starched cap rising
like a Roman arch, cap of the Franciscan order—
or maybe to my sister, or maybe to me.

The accordion, I concluded, was the instrument
of high romance, the instrument of fathers
who trusted their arms, the arms we tested
as he held them out in a crucifixion pose,
one for each daughter to swing from. That
is all I knew about adoration.

2

Dressed in white satin shirts with bloused sleeves,
the kind Zorro wore on TV, cummerbunds
I imagined red in the black and white
photograph, and black satin pants
with a fringed stripe climbing each leg,
they posed with their accordions and a sign—

scrolled in fancy script I recognized as my father's,
for I had seen him down at the drugstore
with jars of red paint and the sign painter's
brushes he flashed across white paper
to announce deep discounts on remedies
for heartburn, pinkeye, bunions, and gout,
all the missteps of the body. But then
they were young, their Cisco Kid hats
set at jaunty angles, ball fringe
dangling from the brims, the three of them kneeling
with their accordions at their knees
adoring as children, or lambs
nuzzling Jesus on the high murals
I dreamed myself into each Sunday
at the Missouri Synod Lutheran Church
while the pastor droned about sin and redemption.

It was Ray who went out to the farm in Uten
where my father was cultivating corn,
Ray who jumped up on the tractor beside my father
and rode three times around the field
talking up the contest over in Chatsworth
before he convinced him to forget
his German upbringing, the plotted ground,
and leave the tractor steaming in the field,
leave the job half done. After "Harbor Lights,"
"Blue Hawaii," "Indian Love Call," and
"Tango of the Roses," they waltzed off the stage
slapping the $25 prize in their pockets. Beautiful
Helen Zalucha led them through a few good
Polish polkas in the band shell at Miller Park
and, still teenagers themselves, they played
high school assemblies where girls swooned
over satin and fringe, the spine-tingling

reverberations of three accordions in sync
moaning out love's whole sultry repertoire.
This was the 1930s, The Decade of the Accordion,
before Paul married a different Helen,
Ray married Priscilla,
and they launched my generation.

3

How willingly ten fingers
accept the task
of melody and chord,
yet the bellows wait like lungs
for measured air,
for hands already full
to orchestrate
give and take.

This my father knew
when he knelt beside me,
taking the weight
in his own hands
to help me try.
The bellows balked and whined,
collapsed like fish
on land, although
I'd seen the pleats open
and fold with the ease
of a Japanese fan
or a woman's skirt in motion
as she twirled across the polished floor
toward the open arms
of Fred Astaire.

Confused, unsynchronous
in my small hands,
the accordion hoarded
music's mysteries,
a reprimand that turned
me back to the childhood
I tried too young to leave.

4

On the first snowy black and white TV of my childhood,
Ed Sullivan clapped for the occasional accordion
act. I was indignant, knowing my father belonged
on that stage. But the year Elvis appeared,
guitar slung like a pelt over one shoulder,
my sister and I looked up from our Betty Grable
paper dolls in time to see him bow, his wavy hair
unpleating like an accordion gone berserk,
and suddenly I divined why father played in the rec room,
and only for his daughters.

The night my mother took me
to the grade school gym to see the instruments
laid out like corpses on long tables,
there was no accordion. "Choose," my mother
said, pointing at the high-polished brass
and chrome contraptions, mysterious as engines,
threateningly mathematical, even though she knew
my one pleasure was evenings locked
in the bathroom with *Gone with the Wind*
where I rewrote the ending so Rhett and I
would be in love forever we were so right
for each other. "Clarinet," I said, reading
the name from a little card propped

in front of it. "Clarinet," I repeated,
without conviction, without knowing
what unimaginable sounds would fall
from the Pandora's box of the tube holes
pressed open, for my child's instinct
assured me my notes would, in fact, fall
instead of rising like angels into the music
of heaven. "Clarinet," I muttered a third time,
reasoning it was almost small, almost
feminine, but saner than the flute, my second choice,
because it stayed out front where it belonged,
where you could watch it with two eyes.
In any case, there'd be a uniform,
a satin shirt like Rhett's on the theatre
marquee, a flouncy skirt, white fringed boots,
a long-billed hat with chin strap,
perhaps a plume, not to mention the breasts
and shapely calves they'd issue with it—
I'd seen the girls on TV.

Clinging to these consolations, I trudged
to the grade school music room
and took my place in the last wooden folding chair
at the end of the row. It tested my faith,
believing this band of surly children
adept at abusing music
could transform cacaphony into "Moonlight and Roses"
or "The Beer Barrel Polka." For days
I waited for the miracle,
still flat chested in my simple cotton shirt,
my legs still spindly under plain black
slacks (not even a stripe), half listening
to dour Mr. Hunicutt repeat how to snap
the sections into place and suck the reed
of this spitty instrument (the only feat
I ever mastered), how to tense my cheeks
and blow until my jaws ached
building muscles in my face

I knew even the most sincere kiss
would bounce right off of. And oh
deep in my heart I was convinced
that Scarlett would have disapproved.

5

Because mothers were supposed to teach
their daughters grace, civility,
appreciation of the genteel life,
my mother, a few years after The Month
of the Clarinet, took my sister to music night
in the grade school gym. A short husky child
who knew her mind, she needed no urging
to embrace the tuba, chosen, I figured,
because it most resembled her.

Framed by our living room window, she trudged
the long block home after band practice
between snowdrifts taller than she was,
her breath trapped in the red muffler
she wore like a mask across her nose and mouth.
Occasionally she'd gallop a bit,
moving to the music of hooves in her head,
pretending, I knew, to be Silver or Buttermilk
or any one of the ceramic horses
trotting across the shelf above her bed.
But it was hard, galloping,
the tuba strapped on her back,
that great hump of noise and sorrow
which splintered the antebellum dreams
I conjured nightly in the bathroom. What good
a lock against those terrible moans?
Shut up in the Midwest, half buried in winter,

the magnolias froze on the branches
of my imagination. It was then, during
The Week of the Tuba, I admitted my desire
to be an only child.

So no polka. No march. But after a brief stint
with the baton between tap, ballet, and acrobatics,
our last-ditch effort at costumes,
we each in turn settled down at the piano
to travel through the mournful bass
of "In the Hall of the Mountain King,"
extinguishing childhood note by note.

6

No one could have known
it would come to this:
father after midnight
planting crab apple saplings
in my backyard,
floodlight propped on a ladder,
cicadas yammering
their single insistent note
he called applause,
so unnameable was his desire
for flowering, so unappeaseable
those manic cells
ricocheting in his brainpan
like shrieks escaped
from a clarinet
sometimes dying into the tuba's
dull blub, the sound
of something huge
going down for the third time.

It was the racket
that drove him
far from the accordion's
rhythmic squeeze,
called him closer
to the crazy music
of despair.

7

My daughter, who long ago quit Grieg
in favor of Tcherepnin's atonal compositions,
called her grandfather's accordion queer,
funky, obsolete. "Look in the Yellow Pages,"
she said. "What's listed under *A*?"
"This is a small town," I explained, understanding
her age forced her to adore Guns N' Roses, and anyway by then
the black accordion with the diamond-studded
button, the mother-of-pearl inlay, had been traded
for a red marblized-plastic number,
a new generation machine harboring no trace
of Paul, Helen & Ray in its history.

She came of age in a world without accordions,
without a father, or even a sister, a world
where Sundays were like every other day.
She grew up with a mother who read in the kitchen,
lost in the music of language,
oblivious to dinner scorching on the stove,
the blue air drifting
toward her child stalled at the piano,
searching out the notes of the future
on a keyboard that asked only one task of each hand.

The Cisco Kid, Rhett, and Fred Astaire,
the embraceable sheet music women, photogenic
Helen Zalucha, all the dreamy filigree of my childhood
vanquished to the fringe of memory.
But still they hover like vapor
above this daughter, their miraculous hands
fanned at her shoulders like wings,
blessing her down the long path of the future,
guiding her toward whatever music
will finally speak to her.

III

The class listens to me
but watches the interpreter
who watches the girl
for whom sight is sound.
I begin with the word
listen. As in "Listen
to the long *O*'s
accruing like sighs,
the sibilant *S*'s
in secrets beginning
with *she.*"
But in her language,
the alphabet
is knuckle and bone,
quick as a fist
or deliberate
as thumb and forefinger
closing to show
"smaller and smaller."
The hands drop
when I conclude,
". . . and then
there was nothing."
I think about
writing without a pen,
a sailboat becalmed,
the top car rocking
on the shut-down Ferris wheel.
The girl smiles
seconds after
my slight jokes.
Her hands are quiet

when I ask for questions.
Together we travel
the poem's bright thread, watch
its beautiful
unraveling.

Slipped

I saw the new Moon,
with the old Moon in her arms
—*Anonymous*

She does not call it the moon
when first she glances up,
believing she sees it whole, full,
right where it should be,
low in the east. Usual coin,
precise medallion, so

why does she look again,
again lift her eyes, risking
the ice-patched road?
When she reaches her destination—
for she has one—
she will not tell her friends
who wait with their arms open
what she has seen. Instead
they will speak of a castrato in Spain
who nightly sang the insomniac king
into the white sleep he desired,
the stupidity of sheep huddled
beneath the electrocution tree—
how they dropped like dominoes.

She snaps on the dome light
and moves well lit
through the terrible cold
past fields where sharp-edged stalks
erupt like bone,
toward the winding drive already shoveled clear,
the forested house where already,
far back in their throats,
the others shape the conversation. So

49

how could she introduce the moon,
say she saw it full
each time her amazed eyes
relinquished the road?
Someone might have said
the sliver completed itself like phantom pain,
then perhaps the others would agree
and she alone would argue no,
defending the two moons
she had seen
one over the other
like a slipped coin laid on an eye,
the visible white crescent
belying the whole, or the daughter
who stands behind her mother
but each year grows.

Childhood Friend, Thirty
Years Later

The young girl inside you remains
unchanged. Or at most there is a subtle
turning, like shifting a wrist for a sly
look at your watch. Such gestures
do not mean older, but deeper,
a hand traveling an octave lower.
The you inside you is kin

to flesh, the other side
of the story, no longer pretty,
that shoulders the extra weight,
complains at irritations in the bone,
protests the skin loosening like wallpaper.

A short list of what the body keeps:

      Fingerprints, invisible as names
      Regular moons studding the base of each nail
      Irises, a persistent shade of blue
      Scars like the one I have carried

for thirty years—two teeth across,
one down, a skeleton key to the past.
As a child you were a biter,
understanding even then how the flesh relents.

The young girl remembers
her girlhood, gives you away
when you lift the knuckle of your index finger
to push your glasses higher on your nose.
So now there are two of you,

a simple problem in multiplication
predicting how on the last day
the old woman will take the girl's hand
as she travels past her, beyond
embryo, egg, their mother undressing,
toward whatever you were and will be.

The Wife Takes a Child

A woman buys a house built long before she was born. One day she goes to inspect the empty rooms where she will live alone. When she walks to the center of the white living room, the bright walls and ceiling make her feel small, weightless, as if she has stepped into a faded family photograph. She plans how she will arrange her sofa and chairs, where she will hang the portrait of her grandparents dressed in their wedding clothes.

Each time she takes a step, another step resounds on the bare floor, a readable map, telling where others crisscrossed the room, stopping at the front window to watch the neighborhood wake up or fall asleep. Two deep grooves where the bench slid to and from the piano explain how much music the house holds.

When the woman crosses to the fireplace, she glances over her shoulder to see if anyone is following her. She kneels at the hearth and reconstructs the ash as headlines announcing the Crash and Pearl Harbor, letters beginning *Dear John* and *I regret to inform you,* playing cards— a marked deck.

For her, they appear in their outdated clothes: the sisters who didn't speak to each other for thirty years, the man who taught his wife to fear him, the man who had no wife at all, the baby that died at birth. Even though she barely recognizes them, the woman knows she will invite them to her table. She takes the squalling baby and offers it her breast then chooses the man with the saddest eyes to carve the meat and pour the rare red wine. After the meal they will remain to confess until the whole house echoes *sorry, sorry, sorry.*

In the Theatre

Music Box, Chicago

By degree the lights go down
like falling temperatures, the slow
descent of sleep. For the previews,
the ceiling stars stay lit—
small proof there is a world beyond
the screen. The cloud machine pumps airy veils
across the painted sky.

              When the film begins
my life retreats like a bird unseen
beneath the eaves. The actors
are not actors but two angels back on earth.
One is tempted by desire
to stay. The aerialist he seeks
aspires to a higher state
and on that middle plane
they meet.

            In his booth, the projectionist
reads the Sunday *Trib*—the Virgin
has appeared to seven girls
in Yugoslavia. First Lourdes,
he thinks, Fatima and now this.
They see her on a hill behind a house,
in the village church, in uncluttered childhood
where visions are routine. He imagines
pilgrims waiting for the cross to spin,
the sun to change its color,
for simple beads to alchemize.
Glancing at the screen
he sees the shadow of the angel's hand
pass through an actual hand

and thinks of two clocks chiming slightly
out of sync.

        Beside me in the flickering dark
a shoulder presses mine—
flesh over bone
resurrects the world again.

HER LIFE WITH CHOPIN

She was born to study piano,
conceived (her mother says) at an hour
when the sultry August air
should have been still, not raging with mazurkas
on the upstairs neighbor's
radio. (Once her father stopped to thump
the ceiling with a broom.) He cursed Chopin.

But she grew up in love with Chopin.
Her father bought her a grand piano.
He likes to think he's paid the neighbor
back as he savors all the endless hours
she requires to memorize her first mazurka,
an adaptation, but still the atonal air

assaults the neighbor overhead who airs
complaints against all pianos and Chopin.
Beating his breakfast eggs in mazurka time,
the neighbor thinks the piano's
in his head. Unstrung, he haunts the hours
the girl pretends her pillow is Chopin. The neighbor

thinks of moving to another neighborhood,
of starting over where air is only air,
where everyone prefers the pleasure of an hour
alone to an obsession with Chopin,
the peace of tea and solitaire to pianos,
the rhythm of the seasons to mazurkas.

Yes, his would be a world without mazurkas
or spiteful fathers or studious neighbor

girls who practice piano and practice piano
until their fingers manufacture airy
romances of finding Frédéric François Chopin
in the passing decades, days, and hours,

always believing in the elusive hour
when lost in the perfect mazurka
the knock at the door will be Chopin,
not an interruption by the neighbor
who means to ask (a feeble trick) *Come out for air?*
The keyhole frames her rapt at the piano.

What the neighbor never understood at any hour
is that a life spent at the piano with Chopin
carves the soul from air to dance the heart's mazurka.

THE FAT GIRL SWIMS THE 500

Humped like a walrus
on the starting block
she's awkward
all lumps.
The crowd has its doubts.
At the gun she flops
with a crack
like rock striking rock
then sinks.

The surface breaks.
She rises
from a sea of swimmers
neck and neck.
The water directs
the language
of fingers and wrists
pull and flick
the rub of thigh on thigh.
Lap after lap
lungs barely taxed
she takes the lead.

Some girls swim
against each other
some the clock.
When she passes them
face to face
one is herself
she leaves behind.

ASKING THE HORSE

Ask with your hands,
calves, with all the bones of your body
engaging and disengaging
to guide him into tight circles
and across the long diagonals
of pleasure and work.

Your hands chamber the questions.
Closed on the reins, they repeat
the angle of his withers,
those steep slopes falling away
from the crest you ride.

Your calf is a post he bends around,
simplifying the world
which is everywhere.

Sky, mountains, the distant
bay: this is the stunned scenery
you must rise above. If

he hesitates, tell him *noblesse oblige*
and ask each pound of the one thousand
to remember his lineage—the great
wars of Europe, far Arabia.
Ask again, tender, deferential,
until you agree on everything.

The Stretch

Bit by bit the past slips
out of her grip. She can no longer
remember which bones she has broken,
languages she once spoke,
places she's lived, whatever she's loved.

Her world is a mat, 3 x 7,
on which she stretches.
She sits and bends her head
down toward her knees. Reluctant,
ill at ease, the muscles balk
and sting, retract, then slip and catch.
Like vines, she coaxes them past
the shape they have come to love.

This is an act called patience,
like watching lines deepen in a face
or the slow branch thicken.
Love grows that way, suddenly
astonishing the future.

In front of her, a wall of windows
invites her eye across the lake's breakable
surface. Her toes point toward the opposite poles
of north and south, she faces east.
Open, she risks the ache she leans into.
Deep in its underwater cage,
her heart begins its long ascent
up the stony elevation of her ribs,
then settles near the surface,
within reach.

Black Dog

In my dream a hand appears, fragile
as a flower unfolding on the forearm's long stem.
Such a hand has memorized
the vocabulary of want and need,
the *please* and *help me*
it cannot trust the mouth to speak.
In one slow-motion frame after the next,
the hand, replete with asking,
performs its studious dance. Finally
I understand the hand is mine.

The inevitable happens: your hand
suddenly revealed. I know it
by the scar across the palm,
twenty stitches neat as tracks.
I think *stigmata,* for the ecstatic wounds,
long stanched, stitched shut,
but no less the injury for that. And *stigma,*
for the three-fingered part of the pistil
rising like an open hand among the anthers,
the part that holds and fosters the tiny grains
of pollen. When our fingers interlock,
I believe there is nothing as sexual
as two hands.

With one finger I trace the scar
down toward its origin near your wrist
then press my palm against your palm.
The thick ridge burns like a brand
forcing me to dream your dream
about a black dog who nuzzles your hand,

takes it into her mouth and swallows,
swallows again, swallows it down
deeper into her throat until she chokes.

THE ECSTASY OF ST. THERESA

after Bernini

If two fingers
could lift her from the world,
they would be his, this boy angel's,
standing above her,
thumb and forefinger
hooking the fabric of her habit.
Already one bare foot
has slipped from the stony shelf
on which they balance.

Twisted toward him, her body's
no longer lost in the abundant drape
pulling now against the seemly curve
of hip and thigh so long concealed,
the rounded calf. Her left knee
dimpled by a stone
alerts the nerves to martyrdom.

All her life she has prayed
for this moment, rising like an island,
lush, weedy, suddenly unveiled,
the full-fleshed domain
of Discipline's unruly daughter.

Dropped back, her head
tests the wimple's give and stretch,
slackens her marble jaw,
prompts her bee-stung lips
to part as for a kiss,
draws down her lids
on the imp who tips into the unaccustomed

weight of wings, his arrow poised
above gravity's sweetest center.
If its flight is direct,
it will enter her without a wound.

Deep Sex

Deep sky is, of all visual impressions,
the nearest akin to a feeling.
—*Samuel Coleridge*

The sky opens its irresistible arms
saying, *You will remember me*
as deeper than sleep. The beginning,
for there is one, is always simple:
a prairie edged with trees that close
like a door behind you.
The path rises and falls like the body
of a woman, a man, then suddenly branches.
Stay calm, the sky counsels,
there is no need to choose,
you can follow them all at the same time
and here there is no such word as lost.
Soon you are so deep
reason disappears like a bird into thick foliage,
daily life stalls,
your daughter's face blurs
although you swore you would never forget her.
Is this the time to mention the man
nearly double your weight
who travels inside your body,
the exchange of breath,
or the tremors that mock the branch
where the flown bird lit?
If you care to look, you will see nothing,
but this you already know
as you know his eyes have deepened
to a certain shade of green you willingly enter
as if it were a place.
You feel there is no end to this:
you feel it as a violet sky
burning down the edges of the Earth,
you feel it pathless, rolling like prairie

65

past the shallow islands of the clouds,
out past every undiscovered planet,
you feel it as a failure of language,
as absence, deep space
that offers the eye no place to stop.

High Image Therapy

At night she lies in bed still as a stone, listening to her heart. The moon outside her window casts shadows of blown branches across the paper shade. Still bare, the smaller limbs pulse like tributaries, traversing the larger ones in an impossible tangle.

Minnows slip along the edge of a childhood stream. Dipping her hands in the water, she holds them as in a cup. Released, they zig-zag like the set fires of fishermen lighting the shores of the great lake every night of the smelt run in early spring. They cast their long nets and haul in thousands of silver fish. Random and beautiful, they thrash themselves still. In the distance, flames flash like fins, wings.

The horse takes the bit in his teeth. Wild, willful, groomed for speed, he is a horse for whom *Stop* means nothing, *Please* means nothing in his language. Hurdling fallen trees, dodging low-hung branches, he is oblivious to the rider and his own heart steady as a clock. She lifts her hands from the bed as if to take up the reins worn smooth, shiny as a razor strop, and works the bit from side to side, coaxing him down to a canter, a trot, a slow high-stepping walk.

The Absence of Edges

to Lisel Mueller

When the sea
seals itself around one ankle,
the rest is history.
Some believe the bottom drops suddenly away,
a confounding absence,
but the slope's seduction
is gradual as sleep.
So I cannot say when
my view of the world shifted,
when I became another horizontal,
a floating middle plane
between sky and sea,
or how for the first time
the world felt complete
as if I were the found piece
of the largest puzzle
consoled at last
by the absence of edges.
Nor can I say when
I looked down through the salt-sting
at whole tribes of sea urchins,
their poison spines
longing for the softest part of me
or at the jewfish whose huge bulk
sulks along the bottom,
stomach round as a diving bell,
but perhaps it was then I understood
they had their own lives
fixed at depths they could not leave
like performers held by the ring,
the stage, the high trapeze.

Crossing the reef to open sea,
I drop one foot to test my luck
against the cruel branches,
draw it back uncut,
admire its rise to the surface,
obedient fish, auspicious,
following me beyond the coral range
into the underwater world
that opens its undulating arms—warm,
forgiving, so perfect
the difference between *escape*
and *narrow escape* means nothing:
that is what I am thinking
when the speck that is me
disappears over the horizon
and although I know I never mean to return
I glance toward shore
imagining the speck that is you
waving in despair,
unable to tell you I am
delivered at last into a country
where everything is the same
shade of blue, where *beginning*
and *end* are not words I use,
where I require no luggage
and hold all conversations with myself,
where the body surrenders its familiar
weight, and gratitude is boundless.

DATE DUE